HOW TO
RELAX
AND UNWIND

igloobooks

igloobooks

Written by Belinda Campbell
Designed by Dave Chapman
Edited by Bobby Newlyn-Jones

Copyright © 2019 Igloo Books Ltd

An imprint of Igloo Books Group,
part of Bonnier Books UK
bonnierbooks.co.uk

Published in 2019
by Igloo Books Ltd, Cottage Farm
Sywell, NN6 0BJ

Manufactured in China. 1119 001
10 9 8 7 6 5 4 3 2 1

Library of Congress Cataloging-in-Publication
Data is available upon request.

ISBN 978-1-83852-538-5
IglooBooks.com
bonnierbooks.co.uk

Introduction

Reduce your everyday stresses and bring
relaxation into your life with these peace-seeking
pages. Whether you have an hour or less than a
minute, this dip-in mindfulness guide will help you
find those precious moments in which to
unwind during your busy day.

There's no expensive online course to sign
up for and you're not told to purchase any
extra accessories. Simply start your journey of
self care by opening this book at random for a
quick and easy technique, exercise, or activity
to complete, then revisit activities which work
for you. If you're really short on time, pick out
a calming phrase or two.

Wake up with a soothing breathing exercise,
experiment with an on-the-go meditation, or close
your day with a reflective writing exercise and
feel yourself begin to relax more easily.

Cleanse the airways

Nadi Shodhana is a cleansing yoga breathing practice that can help reduce tension in the mind and bring a calm focus to your day. Find a seated position where you are comfortable and upright with your back nice and tall.

Take a moment to notice your breath. Now, drop your index finger and your middle finger to your palm. Place your thumb over your right nostril and breathe through your left nostril. Gently pause your breath while you move your thumb away and place your ring finger over your left nostril and breathe out through your right nostril. Keep your ring finger over your left nostril and inhale. Place your thumb over your right nostril, exhale through your left nostril, and repeat.

In simpler terms, switch nostrils each time you breathe in so that you breathe out through the opposite nostril. Finish this breathing practice by taking a big inhale through both nostrils and release any final tensions with an audible breath out through the mouth.

Don't rush your journey;
it decides your destination.

Paint the Town Placid

Art galleries can be incredibly soothing places to visit, but if you don't have one accessible to you then try this exercise with an art book with large photographs instead.

Begin by finding a painting that instills a sense of calm within you. Perhaps it is the colors or the subject that attracts you to it. Now imagine yourself as the artist, channel the focus needed to have made this artwork. Imagine each brush stroke layering upon one another until the painting is complete.

Try to channel this calm focus whenever you are trying to complete a long and tiring task.

New year, New you?

Instead of worrying about coming up with resolutions for ways to be better in the new year or next week, look back on the last day, month, or even longer. On the next page, make a list of all the things that you have accomplished already.

However big or small, be sure to list everything, from changing a tire to paying the bills.

Read back over your list of recent achievements and be proud of each one. Take this moment to relax and maybe give yourself a little reward for everything you have achieved so far.

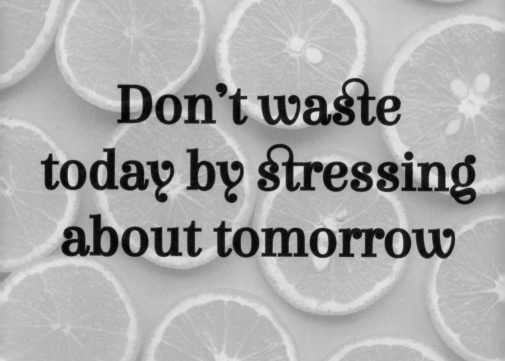

Don't waste today by stressing about tomorrow

THE MINDFUL MUNDANE

For those simple tasks that have you snoozing your way through them (and thinking about whether you sent that email or not), try approaching them in a more mindful manner. By focusing wholly on the task at hand — the more boring the better — the monotony of the mundane can help bring a calm clarity to your mind and have you ready to tackle the rest of your day with a more relaxed focus.

Next time you are loading the dishwasher or brushing your teeth, try to make the mundane meditative and enjoy the relaxing effects.

Bee Calm

Bhramari, also known as the humming bee breath, can transport you to relaxing spring days.

Begin by relaxing your forehead, jawline, neck, and shoulders. As with any breathing exercise, do what feels comfortable and never force your breath or body beyond its personal capability.

Inhale through your nose, keeping your mouth gently closed. Exhale through your nose and begin to make a gentle humming sound. Cover your ears softly with the tips of your index fingers (do not put your fingers inside your ear). Inhale through the nose and repeat as before.

Feel the comforting vibrations travel through you and melt away tension.

Accept Change

Change can be a trigger for disturbing a lot of people's calm. Try this visualization to help you accept a change in your life that is bringing you stress.

Begin by standing or sitting - if your balance is a bit wobbly then try this one sitting down. Notice how your feet are connecting with the floor and let this sensation of touch be the root of your visualization.

Once you are feeling grounded, visualize a beautiful mature tree. Let the trunk, steadfast and secure, remind you of the importance of stillness. Let the bending branches remind you that flexibility is important for growth. Imagine the leaves, changing and falling and growing anew. Let this tree remind you that change can be as beautiful as it is inevitable.

Conjure this tree whenever you need to, as a reminder of the importance of accepting change.

Take a break!

as many as

YOU WANT

and whenever

YOU NEED THEM

VISIT YOUR HAPPY PLACE

In the spaces below, write a few places that make you feel calm.
Notice if there is a pattern to these places. Are they mostly outside?
Are you on your own in these places or with other people?
Now that you have identified a few of these places and why you find them
relaxing, work out how you can regularly visit them to make sure you are
keeping your level of calm topped up. Open your calendar and organize a
day to go and visit one of your happy places now!

ACCEPT BIG

worry little

Write down the one big thing that is bringing you stress.

....

....

....

....

Now, try to think of one thing you can accept about it – just one, start small.

Take traffic as an example. Begin by accepting that 'I need to drive places.' Once you have found one thing to accept, find another, like 'other people need to drive places too.'

Keep going with this exercise until you can see the thing causing you stress begin to change shape as your acceptance of it becomes bigger and your worries over it shrink.

DON'T BE AT WAR WITH THE WORLD.
INSTEAD, FIND YOUR PLACE
WITHIN IT.

Sometimes, to open the door to an instantly calmer you, all you need to do is take a long deep breath.

Begin by noticing your breathing as it currently is and taking three of these regular breaths. Now take the longest and deepest breath you have taken all day, before letting it all out with a relaxing and audible sigh. As you exhale, feel your shoulders drop and your face muscles soften.

Treat yourself to as many of these freeing breaths as you like.

TURN THE VOLUME DOWN ON THE VOICES BRINGING YOU PAIN.

DE-STRESS IN TEN SECONDS

Counting to ten is a tried and tested calming method that many people find helpful, but when you add the benefits of mindful breathing into the exercise it can be even more soothing.

Take a deep breath in on the count of 'one' (it's easier to count in your head so as not to interrupt with the breath) and on 'two,' take a long exhale. Repeat by breathing in on 'three,' exhaling on 'four,' and so on. On your last exhale on 'ten,' feel your mind and body working in better harmony.

AL DESKO MEDITATION

Be able to find your calm whenever and wherever you most need it, including at your desk If your work doesn't have you at a desk, try to find somewhere to sit for five minutes before you try these meditation steps.

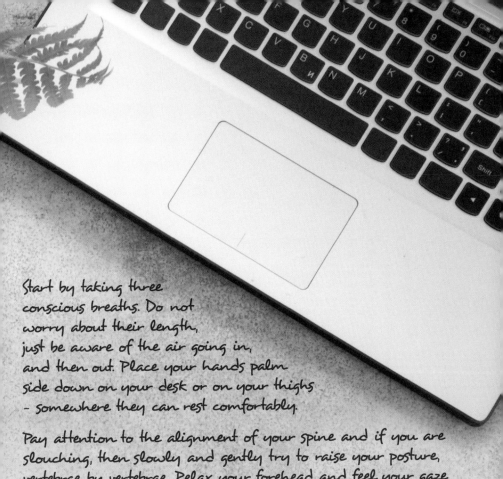

Start by taking three
conscious breaths. Do not
worry about their length,
just be aware of the air going in,
and then out. Place your hands palm
side down on your desk or on your thighs
– somewhere they can rest comfortably.

Pay attention to the alignment of your spine and if you are
slouching, then slowly and gently try to raise your posture,
vertebrae by vertebrae. Relax your forehead and feel your gaze
soften as you do.

Close your meditation with three more conscious breaths and
find yourself calmer and ready to return to your work.

1 Thing at a time

Give yourself a break from worrying about everything all at once. Instead, write down just one thing that has been bringing you the most amount of stress that you would like to improve in your life today.

....

....

....

....

....

Once you have identified this one thing, work out just one way in which you could improve it.

....

....

....

....

....

....

....

....

....

....

Make this your main objective for today and focus
on achieving it before you do anything else.
Instantly, feel the relaxing effect of tackling your
problems more productively.

THAT PEACEFUL PLACE

Think about the last time you were your most relaxed self. Once you have thought of a time and place in your life, write down a list of reasons why that period of your life was peaceful. Was it the people you were with or the activity you were doing?

Look at the list that you have come up with and consider ways in which you could replicate those things in your life today to bring more peace and relaxation back into your present.

TEASE AWAY TENSIONS

Ease up your tension by finding the funny. Take yourself to the cinema to watch a comedy, watch clips of funny animals online, or ask if anyone in the room with you now has any jokes.

As you give yourself over to the lightness of laughter, feel the tension in your shoulders being shrugged off and a spring put back into your step.

YOU DON'T HAVE TO DO IT ALL

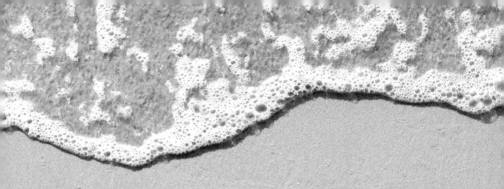

Transport Yourself

The Ujjayi Breath, also known as the ocean breath because of the soothing sounds that your body makes with this exercise, can calm your mind by transporting you to sunny days by the water's edge.

Start by sitting comfortably, and roll your shoulders up and back. Begin to deepen your breath, inhaling through the nose and exhaling with a soft audible 'haah' through your mouth as if you are fogging up a window pane with your breath. Feel a slight contraction in the back of your throat which transforms your breath into the soothing sound of the ocean. When you are comfortable with this gentle tightening in the back of the throat, close your mouth and continue the exercise by breathing in through the nose and out through the nose.

Try to continue making the sounds of the ocean with your mouth now closed. Stay mindful to the sound of your breath and feel your worries drift further and further away from you.

The gift of giving

Use part of your time today to do something for someone else. Whether it's helping a neighbor to get their shopping, volunteering at a local shelter, or cooking a meal for a friend, choose to go out of your way to help someone who needs it.

The joys of giving to someone else rarely fails to make both the giver and the recipient feel better, so try and tap into this giving mindset often to ensure that you and your surrounding world are both happy and at peace.

Take a day off

Sometimes stress can build up when we start to feel trapped in a cycle of continuous work.

Review your work and personal calendars and find a day that you can take off for just you. Avoid making plans with other people on this day and do something that you have always wanted to do – it might be visiting a place you have always wanted to go to or just spending an entire day streaming movies!

Whatever it is, do something that you are usually too busy to do and enjoy the relaxing effect of taking a well-deserved break!

Switch off stress

As you fall into bed and stressful thoughts enter your head it can be hard to drift off into a restful sleep.

Think of yourself in a room where each thought you have is a light bulb. As each thought enters your mind, turn it off by flicking a light switch. When other thoughts or even the same thought keep entering your mind, continue to switch them off one flick at a time.

Feel the room you are in become dimmer, until you find yourself wrapped in a soothing darkness that enables you to drift into a more restful state.

Don't suffer twice by stressing over something that hasn't happened yet

COOL OFF

Sitali Pranayama is a yoga breath,
perfect for times when you need to chill out.

Come to a relaxed seated position that allows your spine to
find length. If you can, roll your tongue. If you can't do this,
don't worry, simply place your tongue loosely through your lips.

Take a long cooling breath in through the mouth and hold gently for a pause of two seconds. Close and relax your mouth so that your tongue is no longer rolled or sticking out and finish your breath by exhaling through your nose.

Repeat as many times as you like, whenever you feel the need to cool off.

A Peaceful Pause

For a quiet recharge that doesn't require remembering any certain breathing steps or mantras, this calming practice is simple but effective.

Take yourself somewhere where you will not be disturbed for the next minute or two. When you are alone, close your eyes and draw your focus to your breathing. Feel each breath go in and each breath go out. Let your body take over and do the hard work – you are simply there to pay attention.

Recharge with this exercise regularly and enjoy a more relaxed you.

ACCEPT WHAT

IS

Continuous Calm

Lying down, take this moment to close your
eyes and tap into how your body is feeling.
Notice your breathing.
Are you holding it in places?
Or taking short inhales?

Now that you are tuned into your breathing,
you can begin. Try to relax as each new
breath begins and ends.

Imagine your breath is a tide, going in and out.
Smooth and continuous and without the need
for pause. Repeat until you are awash with calm
and your unbroken breath flows more seamlessly
than when you first started the practice.

Let Go Of Stress

If there are anxious thoughts repeatedly racing through your mind, then this breathing exercise can help you find some release.

Adopt a position where you can comfortably take deep breaths, whether that's seated, standing, or lying down. Choose what works for you today.

Take hold of one of your anxious thoughts as you take a long inhale through your nose. Now, as you exhale through your mouth, imagine the thought leaving your body.

Repeat as many times as necessary to let go of any stressful thoughts you have been holding on to.

Smell Serene

Awakening your senses can help calm a racing mind and bring you into a relaxed state of the present.

Smell, of all the senses, is generally most closely linked to memory, so try to find a smell that conjures up a relaxing time for you. Find the scent that calms your spirit and keep it close to you. Whenever you need to channel a sense of calm, spritz yourself or your surroundings with your chosen scent and enjoy the memory of peace and tranquility that you have summoned.

Write away a bad day

Write down all the moments of stress that you experienced today, e.g.

- Missed my alarm
- Ran late for a meeting
- Was yelled at
- Didn't get a reply to my message
- Had an unexpected bill

This list will look different for everyone, make it personal to your day.

Look at the parts of your day that have brought you stress and upset. Acknowledge that they have happened.

Now cross them all out, slowly, one by one. As you do, make your exhale last the length of your crossing out and feel the stresses of the day leave you.

Phone a friend

Whoever you thought of when you started reading this page, keep that person in your mind. Don't worry about how long it has been since you last spoke to them, hold onto your instinct of wanting to speak to them and follow it through. Call them up now, ask them how they are, and find out what is going on in their life.

Taking the time and energy to listen to someone else can help you gain perspective of your own problems and allow you to focus on helping someone else through their own.

SITTING COMFORTABLY?

Good, you deserve a rest!

Body Scan

Checking in with your body makes you more aware of your needs and able to identify ways in which you need to relax.

Begin by lying down. Take a moment to get comfortable. Notice the parts of your body that are making contact with the surface that you are lying on, be it a bed, grass, or carpet. Take your awareness to your breath and enjoy a couple of regular breaths or perhaps some belly breaths.

Starting at the tips of your toes, begin mentally scanning your body. Notice how every part of you is feeling today. What are your energy levels like? Are you tired? Is your foot twitching? Are you thirsty? Do you have a headache?

Continue the scan through legs, arms, torso, and face, until you have checked in with your entire self.

When you listen to your body it can often tell you what it needs, so do a regular scan to listen out for what your body is trying to tell you.

Manage Your Emotions

Write a list of the emotions that are currently overwhelming you. Next to each emotion, write a way in which you could reduce feeling that way. This list will be entirely personal to you but here are a few ideas to get you started:

- Feeling angry – try a breathing exercise
- Feeling exhausted – try to go to bed an hour earlier
- Feeling stressed – try taking regular breaks

As you become familiar with the relaxation tips and techniques in this book, begin to write down the names of the exercises which help you manage each of these emotions best.

Got a Minute?

Sixty seconds may not be very long, but sometimes it's all you need to bring you back into a present state of calm.

Firstly, apply some hand lotion to the palm of your left hand and rub in gently with your right thumb. Blend it up each of your left fingers for the first half a minute, then do the reverse on the right hand. Breathe in the scent and feel your hands waking up to the present moment.

This one-minute meditation is so handy and short that you can do it several times a day and keep your inner calm topped up regularly.

If you don't like hand lotion, try the same thing with a bit of hand sanitizer or even with a little soapy water.

Forest bathing

While sunny days may have you running for the beach, heading for the dappled sunshine of trees in times of stress could be a more relaxing refuge.

The Japanese-inspired joy of forest bathing can include reading a book beneath a tree, taking a walk through a forest, or even sitting on a bench in a park. Whether you're bathing yourself in the calming influence of a single tree or a whole forest of them, forest bathing is thought to reduce anxiety, anger and general feelings of tiredness. It's well worth exploring your local area in search of soothing natural spaces.

Find your pieces of peace

Try to identify the core people, places and things that bring you happiness and help you to unwind after a long and hard day. Fill in the blanks below and turn to the answers whenever you need to:

- I feel calm when I _____

- _____ helps bring me peace

- Talking to _____ relaxes me

- My happy place is _____

- I am content with_____

FAN THE FLAMES OF ZEN

Candles are a great way to create a relaxed atmosphere; the smells can inspire our senses, while the soothing light can help soften our gaze and release built-up tension caused by brightly lit offices or screens.

In a safe place, light a candle and give the flame your complete focus. Note how it rises and falls and maybe flickers when you exhale. Take this moment to enjoy its warmth, light and energy.

Watch the flame for a few minutes to restore a sense of calm before taking care to extinguish it at the end of your practice.

Clear the decks

Take a moment to look around your surroundings. Are there dishes that need washing? Does the laundry still need to be put away? Is your desk lost in a week's worth of paperwork?

Wherever you are, try to remove some of the excess mess that is currently cluttering up some of your precious space. Do this in all the rooms and areas in your life that you need to restore some calm and order to.

A Calm Encounter

Caught in a conversation with someone
bringing you stress or triggering your anxiety?

Quietly take your focus to your breathing.
Notice the air flowing into you and out of you.
Try to count the lengths of your breath in your
head if it's not too distracting.

It doesn't take much energy to be mindful of your breath.
Give it just a fraction of your attention the next time
someone is speaking to you. See how your breathing
becomes more even and your attention to the conversation
becomes calmer and more focused.

CHANGE YOUR TUNE

If a meditative state is escaping you and the sound of your own stressed-out voice is too loud to tune out, try listening to soothing sounds or songs. Experiment with sounds of rainfall, birdsong, classical music, or club classics! Find out what works for you to best quieten your stressed-out thoughts.

Create your own peaceful playlist which will help you to find a more meditative state before you start your practice, then simply press play whenever you need to encourage some relaxation.

Take a Reality Break

Daydreamers may get a bad reputation,
but exercising our imagination can be
a powerful stress-busting tool.

Letting your mind wander to a happier,
stress-free place allows you not only to take a
temporary break from a stressful day, but it can
also help actualize your dreams by bringing
them to the forefront of your mind.

When the fancy takes you, allow yourself
a moment to daydream for a few minutes.
Hold onto the ideas and emotions that
you explored in your daydream and try to
bring them into your present.

The right way to write

Writing lists can be a useful and soothing act in itself, but it can also be a procrastination tool used to avoid doing the actual tasks themselves!

Before you begin writing your to-do-list, identify in your mind what is the most important thing that you need to do that day.

Now, write that at the top of your list and make sure it is the first thing you tackle today.

You'll feel calmer straight away from having identified and prioritized today's number one aim and be able to work through the rest of your tasks with a more relaxed focus.

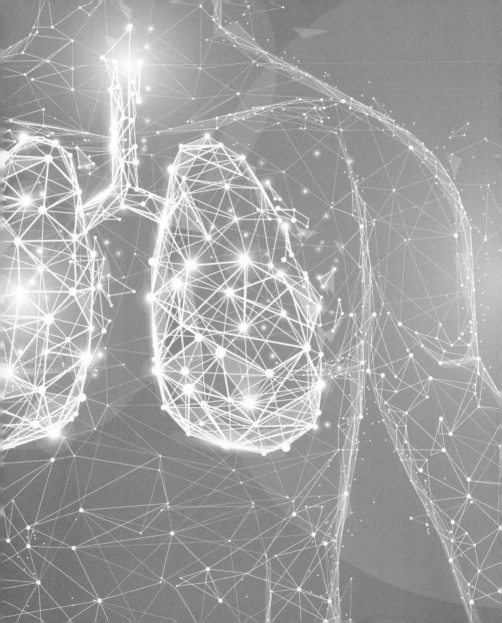

Draw your Breath

Our breathing changes when we are anxious, sad, excited, or scared, and is a clear indicator of our mood. Find the beauty in each of your moods by creating a breathing journal.

For five minutes each day, draw or write the pattern of your breathing: How long is your inhale? How long is your exhale? Does it catch midway?

Get creative with documenting your breath by using numbers, lines, symbols, colors, whatever takes your imagination! Note the emotions attached to each breath, then try to replicate the patterns where you have felt your most relaxed whenever you need a moment.

Results come over time,
NOT OVERNIGHT.

When you are next faced with someone that brings you stress, try focusing on the labels that you have attached to that person. Is it that they are 'rude,' 'a bully,' 'disorganized,' or 'two-faced'? See the labels that you have written sticking to their forehead like a price tag, see the larger ones dangling from their wrists.

Now, try to remove each label that you have attached to them. Try to see that person afresh each day without the stress of these labels. See how your attitude towards that person changes and your interactions with them become more relaxed.

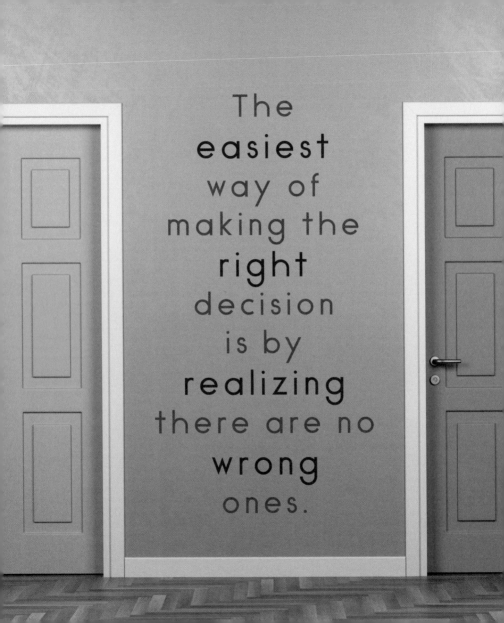

Find your flow

When your emotions are running down, don't try and swim upstream against them. Like nature, let your emotions run their course.

Imagine them like a river. If you are feeling overwhelmed, the waters may be swollen and overflowing; if you are feeling low, your river may look shallow and barely moving; if you are angry then the waters may be racing and thunderous. Remember, you are not a boat trying to balance on these changing waters, you are the waters themselves. These fluid emotions will ebb and flow, and in time they will take you to different shores.

Let them.

Satisfy your needs

Use the space provided to write a list of your needs. Not a list of things that you need to do, but a list of your personal needs. They might include:

- Needing to get more sleep
- Needing to eat healthily
- Needing to take time for myself
- Needing to talk about my emotions

Whatever they are, make yourself pay attention to each and every one.

If you are in the habit of prioritizing the needs of others over your own, try to address that now as you take this moment for realizing your own personal needs and reap the relaxing rewards.

BREATHE WELL, BE WELL

Practice your belly (abdominal) breathing to press your inner reset button and restore relaxation.

Find a calming place to sit or lie down. Place a hand on your stomach, just below your navel. Once you are comfortable, take a long and soothing breath through your nose and feel

the cool air traveling all the way down into your belly.
Feel your hand rise gently as your abdomen expands with
the fresh oxygen. Exhale through your mouth and repeat.

Try to breathe deeply into the belly every day to keep
yourself well looked after and stress-free.

Send stress away

When stressful thoughts are mounting up in your mind, this simple visualization technique can help send them away.

Take a moment to steady your breath and close your eyes to promote a calmer focus. Visualize yourself in front of a mailbox, holding an envelope.

As soon as an unhelpful thought or bad memory rears its ugly head, shrink the thought or person down to the size of your envelope. Place the shrunken problem inside the perfectly fitting envelope and put it in the mailbox in front of you.

Continue to do this with each stress or concern racing through your mind; simply shrink, seal, and mail it. You may find the same stress popping up, but keep shrinking it to the size of the envelope and it will soon become more manageable in your mind.

Soothing Sense Cycles

You can practice this de-stressing tip
anywhere and at any time!

Firstly, take note of where you are
right now. Take in your surroundings, sense
by sense. Look at the space that you are in,
both near and in the distance. Feel each point
of contact that your body is making with
your surroundings.

Take the longest breath you have taken all
day and try to taste the air on your tongue.
As you let it out, listen to the sound of your
breath and any other noises around you.

Repeat each sense as a calming cycle
whenever you need a simple stress relief.

GET TO KNOW THE ISSUE

It can seem easier to ignore our problems than coming face to face with them, but staring our truths straight in the eye can be a surprisingly comforting exercise.

Lay your hands on both this page and a pen while you take three relaxing breaths. As you release your third breath, take the pen in hand and begin to write down a problem in your life.

Try to get to the very heart of it. Be honest with yourself. Admission is part of acceptance and acceptance can help us face our problems more clearly and calmly.

MAKE IT COUNT

Counting your breaths can help bring awareness to your health and emotions, and restore a soothing balance to the mind, body, and soul.

Take one deep breath before you begin your counting. On your next inhale, begin counting (in your head is best).

Stop counting as you feel your lungs reach their full capacity and then start counting down from the number that you reached on your inhale. So, if you breathed in for five seconds, breathe out for five seconds.

Take your time with this one — you may not find the balance straightaway — and let the soothing symmetry emerge slowly.

Don't put baby in the corner

Relax into your emotions with this visualization exercise.

Imagine each of your feelings, your anxiety, excitement, nerves, and happiness, as small babies. Appreciate that neither one is more important or more deserving of your love than another. Each emotion is tender and in need of kindness; each baby needs your attention. Cradle them close, accept their existence, know that they will grow and change, leave you and return to you. Sometimes they will cry or laugh and leave you feeling high or exhausted.

Try to be attentive as a parent to your feelings, and watch them grow and transform.

Say mellow to mantras

Usually a single word or sound recited to promote a calm focus, mantras can be a shortcut to unwinding regularly and quickly.

Think of a calming emotion that you would like to channel today and decide to make it your mantra. It may be 'relaxation,' 'inner-peace,' 'forgiveness,' or 'patience.' Try and keep it to one or two words to make it easy to remember and repeat.

Recall it as you walk through your day or as you focus on your breathing. Think of your chosen mantra throughout your day and make it the background beat to each of your tasks as you tap into its soothing meditative powers.

TOGETHER IS BETTER

Meal times can be a great opportunity to catch up and unwind with our loved ones.

Shake up any solitary eating habits that you may have and strive to make eating a more sociable affair. Try taking the work newbie out for a welcome lunch, catching up with an old school friend, or calling your mom.

Take your lunch breaks to fully recharge and reconnect and be able to continue your day with a more relaxed attitude.

MAKE FUN OF YOUR FEARS

Firstly, make sure you are in a place that you feel safe and calm. Thinking about what brings us fear can trigger some strong emotions, so try this one when you feel relaxed and ready.

Once you are comfortable, begin to visualize one thing that brings you stress. If it is hard to visualize, for instance 'travel,' make your fear take the form of a person or animal that you think best suits it.

Now for the fun part. After you have your fear where you want, you can start to make fun of it; dress it up in silly clothes, paint flowers on its face, make it balance on water skis, or juggle balloons.

When you have suitably entertained yourself, remember this feeling of one-upping your fear for when you next come face to face with it and remind yourself of this private joke to help you relax.

DON'T MIND YOUR MOOD

Emotions are often interlinked with people's moods, but is it possible to feel stressed-out and still try and be in a good mood?

Start by trying to recognize the idea that any emotions you feel are totally normal, natural, and vital for your health and well-being. Tell yourself, 'I feel this way for a reason,' then work out what that reason is.

Understanding ourselves is an important way that you can relax into how you are feeling and become more at ease with our worries.

I Feel

....

....

....

....

....

....

....

....

....

....

....

....

....

....

Because

....

....

....

....

....

....

....

....

....

....

....

....

....

....

SLEEP MORE, STRESS LESS

Lack of sleep can amp up your stress levels. Ask yourself, are you getting less than the usually recommended 7-9 hours? Even if you are within this guidance, try taking yourself to bed one hour earlier than usual.

Ditch the phone and any other screens and replace them with a book to read or a journal to write in. Getting into the habit of reading or writing before bed can help promote a more restful sleep and have you waking up a calmer, fresher you!

SPRING CLEAN YOUR MIND

When your head is feeling cluttered, each of your thoughts will try to convince you of its importance to stay. So how do you decide what needs to go?

Simple: if a thought is making you feel negative, then throw it out!

If it's making you stressed, chuck it away!

Fill a garbage bag with all your unwanted thoughts in this present moment, then tie it up and kick it to the curb. It's easy for trash to pile itself up again, so try and have a clear out regularly – whenever you tidy your desk or bedroom, have a quick mental tidy too.

TAKE A

BREATHER

In times of stress, controlling your breath can help restore calm.

Begin this practice by sitting restfully in a relaxed but upright position. Try to release any tension in your face and jaw. Keep your head facing forward and your chest nice and open.

Inhale deeply through your nose. When you are ready, exhale slowly through softly pursed lips - imagine you are blowing the flame of a candle but trying not to blow it out, keeping your exhale calm and controlled.

Try repeating two or three times until you feel relaxed and ready to continue your day.

✈ Switch on Airplane mode

Mindfulness comes in all forms, shapes, and sizes. One way to find a mindful practice that suits you is to identify what brings you stress and work out how to turn that stress off.

For a lot of people, their phones can be a constant source of pressure, beeping, flashing, and demanding your attention. Whether you think your phone is the route of your anxieties or not, try switching it to airplane mode for an hour. If you're feeling brave, stretch it for two hours!

Do this regularly and feel your anxieties reduce.

LET THE PAINT DRY

To practice both appreciation and patience, try this arty visualization exercise.

Imagine yourself as a blank canvas. Now, begin painting the canvas with things that make you who you are. Try to capture both good and bad memories, like your first break-up and passing your driving test. See it all as brush strokes, color, texture, and beauty. Now sit in front of your painting and allow it to dry. Notice how some areas are drying faster than others.

As you wait for your creation to dry, focus on your breathing while you appreciate the artwork you have created.

STEP MINDFULLY

Step into your present by taking a meditative walk.
There is no need to plan your route or think too
much about where you are going. Simply leave your
door and step outside. With each step you take,
be mindful of how it feels.

Your focus should not be on where you will end up
or how far you have gone, but rather on how the
floor feels beneath your feet, the sounds that your
steps make.

Walking is usually a means of transport to get us
to where we need to go, but it also ignites all the
senses, connects us to our surroundings, and boosts
blood circulation by encouraging us to take deeper
breaths. By focusing on each step taken, you will
find that you are walking at a pace which is probably
slower than what you are used to; try not to resist
this by speeding up.

Tread mindfully and feel the slow pace soothe you.

Consciously Calm

This is a calming practice that requires you to do very little, but can have a huge effect on how we understand and control our emotions.

The aim is simple. Throughout your day, pay attention to your breath – that's it. Simply give it the attention that it deserves as a vital life source. Don't set out to change your breath in any way but quietly pay attention to its natural ebb and flow.

So, whether you're running for the bus, readying yourself for a big meeting, or drifting off to sleep, breathe with intent and feel yourself become more consciously calm throughout your day.

BREATHE OUTSIDE THE BOX

A technique known for its stress-busting results, 'box breathing' is another way that you can try to breathe with intent.

Start in a comfortable seated position, eyes open or closed. Relax your breathing by taking a few easy and even breaths. Begin your box breath by inhaling through your nose for four seconds. Gently hold onto your breath for four seconds, then release it out through your mouth over another four seconds. Pause for four final seconds before beginning your box again and breathing in for another four.

Ease into this practice gently, perhaps building yourself up to holding your breath for the full four seconds. Try blocks of two or three for starters, and always only do what feels good to you.

On one side of the teeter-totter, write a list of all the things you would like to do more of.

On the other side of the teeter-totter, write down all the things you would like to do less of.

....

....

....

....

....

Restore

Once you have finished, assess the balance. Is it right for you? If not, how can you work to adjust it?

As our lives change, this list should alter, so come back to this exercise regularly and make sure that you are achieving the best balance for yourself.

....

....

....

....

....

Balance

Find the next step

Stressing over not
having reached your aims yet?

Write your main aim at the top
of the ladder on the opposite page.

Write the steps you have taken towards your
aim so far on the bottom steps of the ladder.

Now write the steps you need to take
next as you work your way up the ladder.

You may find that you have missed a few necessary
steps on your way to the top, so go back, look at your
ladder, and calmly work out what you need to do next.

Compose Some Calm

With typing being the written norm for most, the physical art of writing can be a relaxing change of pace.

First, start by keeping a pad and pen next to your bed — choose a pen that you particularly like the feel of in your hand and how it glides on the paper.

When your morning alarm goes off, or when you climb into bed, write down a sentence or two. It could be something you heard or felt today. If you are stuck for something to write, copy out a sentence from a book.

Keep at it daily and enjoy the peacefulness of penning.

Free yourself up to forgive

Learn to let go and find peace with the world by taking the time to forgive. Try practicing forgiveness now by completing the sentences below:

- I forgive_____
  for_____

- I forgive myself for_____

- I forgive my_____
  for_____

The more you find yourself holding onto grudges, the more regularly you should practice this writing exercise.

Once you begin to regularly let go of the things that bring you stress, the lighter and more relaxed you will become.

Stick to sticky notes!

If a to-do list is too alarming to look at, try writing down just one task on one small piece of paper.

Take a stack of sticky notes and write down the first thing you need to do today. As you complete the task on the first sticky note, peel it away and place it down somewhere it will not blow away. Continue to write down your next task on a new sticky note and, once finished, add it to your 'completed' pile.

See how many you get through this way by giving each task your calm and undivided focus.

Yours serenely

If you worry about expressing your thoughts or feelings accurately, letter writing can be an effective practice to help you articulate your emotions in your own time.

Firstly, free yourself up emotionally by writing a letter that you do not intend to send. The letter might be addressed to someone or to no one at all. Take your time with writing your letter and when you have finished, sign and seal it in an envelope.

Dispose of the letter whichever way you choose and take relief in knowing that you have said what you needed to say.

PEOPLE

A mindful focus can be easier
to achieve without any distractions,
but learning to stay calm and present
in the busy and noisy everyday world
is a valuable skill to practice.

Crowded places can be a major source of
stress for many people, so learning how
to relax with this mindful exercise can
be a useful trick. Firstly, notice your
breathing, not to change it, but simply
to help you tune into a more
mindful mode.

WATCHING

Next, find a person in the crowd and begin to watch them. Notice what it is about them that caught your eye. List the words that would best describe that person. Think about the colors they are wearing, for example, the fabrics of their clothes, etc. Once you have exhausted one, find another person and do the same.

After repeating this a few times, see if you are now able to navigate through the crowds more calmly.

LIGHTS OUT, BREATHE IN

When we are stressed, it can play havoc with our sleep. For calming your nerves before drifting off into a restful sleep, try this breathing exercise.

Take a few deep breaths before you begin.
On your next inhale begin counting in
your head.

As you reach the end of your inhalation,
add 'one' to the number you reached and
make that the target length of your exhale.
So, if your inhale was two seconds long,
try to exhale for three.

Continue until you can feel your breath
deepening and taking you into a more
relaxing slumber.

Don't sweat the small stuff

Sometimes it's easy to stress out over all the small and annoying things in life, like, 'what am I going to wear today?' or, 'who used all the milk?'

To help minimize these little things disrupting your calm, write down a list of the things that matter most in your life right now.

- My family is fed
- My legs/arms/heart are all working
- I have a roof over my head
- I am getting enough sleep

Writing this down can help you to step out of your stress and remind you not to sweat the small stuff!

THE HEART OF A LION

If you are worried about what others think of you, this breathing exercise can help you leave those fears and worries behind by tapping into a more confident and relaxed you.

Start in a crossed legged pose or with your legs folded beneath you and with your buttocks resting on your heels. Loop your shoulders up and over towards your back, releasing any tension and creating an open space between the ears and the shoulders.

Inhale through the nose and exhale with a hissing 'haaaaah' sound through the mouth. Inhale again and, on your next exhale, take your gaze upwards and stick your tongue out and down.

Take five of these lion breaths and be mindful not to hold any tension in your jaw, neck and shoulders as you repeat. Notice at the end of this exercise how your mind and body feel. This practice can also be soothing if you have been grinding your teeth or experiencing any tightness in the jaw due to stress.

Suspend your expectations

After a while, we all develop certain expectations of ourselves and others, but they can be a source of anxiety when we fail to meet them or feel the need to exceed them.

Start your day with no expectations, aims, or presumptions and approach everything with a new and grateful attitude today. Notice how disappointments fail to attach themselves to you and how you can tackle challenging situations with a lighter ease now that the weight of expectations has been lifted from you!

Let yourself feel sadness, it's no less important than experiencing happiness.

Cast your net further

It's easy to get tangled in your own fears and doubts and lose sight of the bigger picture. Take a moment to look around your surroundings and ask yourself:

- How did these coffee beans arrive in my cup this morning?

- Who chose the paint color for this room?

- Who planted that tree over there?

Reminding yourself that everything is connected in some way can help you feel more at peace in the world. Practice casting your net wide whenever you feel overwhelmed and in need of grounding.

Walk to unwind

Walking is a part of most people's lives, whether it's walking to the car, up and down stairs, or just moving from room to room.

Walking joins each bit of your day together, whether you're taking 10 steps towards the bathroom or 50 steps round the store to buy more milk. Take these interconnecting moments and make them mindful by focusing on each step you take.

Before the day ends, you will have tapped into a present state of mind more than you ever thought practical without having to change your daily routine in any way.

Unwind, Don't Rewind

Bad day? It's easy to replay the terrible moments in our lives, asking ourselves what we could have done differently or what else we could have said in response and how things might have been different.

Think of a scene in a film where things have gone badly for the main character. Did you rewind the film and play the same scene over and over again? Of course not!

Imagine today has been that scene in the movie where things have gone terribly wrong. Play it through once in your mind, just as you remember it all happening. Acknowledge the events of each scene and how they made you, the main character, feel.

Once the scene is over, don't press rewind — let the rest of your movie now play out!

LEARN TO ACCEPT CRITICISM

When taken well, criticism can teach us to grow into better people, when taken badly it can have the reverse effect. When you next hear words of criticism, take a deep breath before you react.

Regardless of how the criticism is given, take control over how you receive it and how you use it. Listen calmly to the words of advice coming your way and use it constructively to make any criticism your ally and not your enemy.

Your calming comrades

Write a list of people in your life that you feel most relaxed with.

....

....

....

....

....

When you have identified your calming comrades, organize some dates to see these peace-filling people.

Once you have reached out to your chosen list, add these contacts into your favorites on your phone and try to stay in contact with them as often as possible, either in person, via letter, email, or over the phone.

Enjoy relaxing with these positive relationships and making your bonds even stronger.

Notes

Use this page to record what works for you, and any other
techniques or strategies you might discover.

....

....

....

....

....

....

....

....

....

....

....

....

....

....

HOW DOES YOUR GARDEN GROW?

By Pat Patterson
Illustrated by Brenda Clark and Debi Perna

 An OWL Magazine/Golden Press Book

©1985 by Pat Patterson. Illustrations ©1985 by Debi Perna and Brenda Clark. All rights reserved. Printed in the U.S.A. by Western Publishing Company, Inc. OWL Magazine is a trademark of the Young Naturalist Foundation. GOLDEN®, GOLDEN & DESIGN®, GOLDEN PRESS®, and A LITTLE GOLDEN BOOK® are trademarks of Western Publishing Company, Inc. Library of Congress Catalog Card Number: 85-70828 Canadian ISBN 0-920775-02-0 U.S. ISBN 0-307-02027-4/ISBN 0-307-60285-0 (lib. bldg.)

B C D E F G H I J

Published in Canada by Greey de Pencier Books, Toronto. Canadian Cataloguing in Publication Data Patterson, Pat. How does your garden grow? ISBN 0-920775-02-0 I. Clark, Brenda. II. Perna, Debi. III. Title. PS8581.A77H69 1985   jC813'.54   C85-098290-1   PZ7.P37Ho 1985

An earthworm was crawling along. Suddenly
the earth around him started to crack and crumble
in a most alarming way.

"Hey! What's going on here?" the earthworm
asked himself. He wriggled his long, pink body
up through the soil to find out.

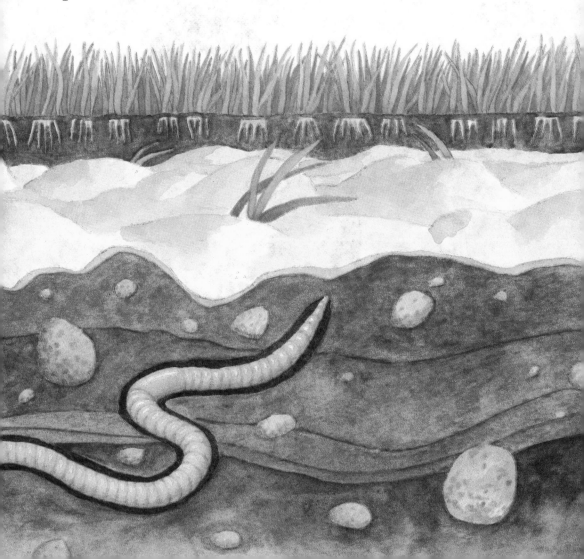

No wonder the earth was moving! Someone was digging with a spade. It was a girl. To the earthworm she looked very big.

The earthworm crawled to a safe corner of the garden. There he was joined by a caterpillar, an ant, and a snail.

The girl, whose name was Gaily, dug, hoed, and raked. Her little brother, Sebastian, helped her.

This was the first time Gaily had ever made
a garden of her very own.

When the earth was ready, Gaily carefully
planted some seeds.

"It's raining!" exclaimed the snail. "I'm going inside my shell to stay dry."

"Oh, dear," said the caterpillar, crawling under a leaf at the edge of the garden. "When my fuzz gets wet I look like a worm. Ugh!"

"Don't be rude!" said the earthworm.

"Actually," the ant announced, "it's *not* raining. That girl is watering the seeds to make them grow."

When Gaily finished watering, she tried to
roll up the hose. By mistake, she got all
tangled up.

Later, a flock of birds flew into the garden. The earthworm was afraid of being eaten. He hid in the soil. But the sparrows ate only seeds.

To frighten away the birds, Gaily and Sebastian made a scarecrow that fluttered in the breeze.

The birds stayed away.

"Hooray! The radishes are up!" shouted Gaily
a few weeks later.

"But those are only green leaves," complained
Sebastian. "Where are the round, red parts?"

"The red parts are under the ground," said
Gaily, wisely. "They need more time to grow."

Later Gaily dug up a radish to see how big it was. The round, red part was too tiny to eat. Gaily put the radish back and packed the earth around it.

As the vegetables grew, so did the weeds.
Some weeds were harder to pull out than others.
Once when Sebastian pulled one out, he toppled
over, just missing the earthworm, the snail,
the caterpillar, and the ant.

One day, Gaily discovered some little green bugs on the tomato plants. She went to her mother for advice.

"Those green bugs are called aphids," Gaily's mother said. "They are bad for plants."

"What a peculiar smell!" exclaimed the ant after Gaily and her mother had planted flowers called marigolds around the tomatoes.

The little green bugs didn't like the marigolds' smell. Soon the aphids were gone.

"Good riddance to bad rubbish," said the earthworm.

"How dare you!" replied the ant. "Some of my best friends are aphids."

The argument grew so fierce that they didn't notice anyone coming.

But Sebastian saw the stranger. He ran to
Gaily. He shouted, "There's a tiger in your
garden!"

Sebastian's family knew he sometimes made things sound bigger than they were. But the family was careful, just in case.

There was no tiger in the garden — just a large ginger cat.

Then came the day that Gaily picked many kinds of delicious, fresh vegetables.

For a while, the earthworm rode on the basket. Then Gaily saw him and put him on the ground.

The earthworm wriggled back into the garden.

As he got there, Gaily and her family gave three cheers. The earthworm thought they were cheering for him, but they were really cheering for Gaily and her wonderful garden.

Hooray!